Bible Story
Color 'n' Learn

Grades PK-1

by
Michelle Medlock Adams

Carson-Dellosa Publishing Company, Inc.
Greensboro, North Carolina

It is the mission of Carson-Dellosa Christian to create the highest-quality Scripture-based children's products that teach the Word of God, share His love and goodness, assist in faith development, and glorify His Son, Jesus Christ.

"Teach me your ways so I may know you."
Exodus 33:13

Credits:
Editor: Ginny Swinson
Cover Design and Illustration: Nick Greenwood
Layout Design: Nick Greenwood
Inside Illustrations: J. J. Rudisill

All scripture quotations, unless otherwise indicated, are taken from the HOLY BIBLE, NEW INTERNATIONAL VERSION®. NIV®. Copyright © 1973, 1978, 1984 by International Bible Society. Used by permission of Zondervan. All rights reserved.

This book contains stories about Bible events. To maintain readability level for the intended audience, the author has paraphrased all stories and quotations within stories. In addition, age-appropriateness was considered when selecting the portions of stories to include. While every effort has been made to achieve a high level of accuracy, the stories in this book are not intended to replace the stories in the Bible. Teachers and parents are encouraged to consult their preferred version of the Bible to clarify stories or portions of stories as needed.

ISBN 978-1-60418-112-8

05-082151151

Table of Contents

Table of Contents

Table of Contents

New Words to Learn!

The Bible stories in this book use prekindergarten to second grade vocabulary with the exception of these words. Each new word also appears at the bottom of the story in which it is used. You may wish to teach these vocabulary words before reading or studying each story.

alive	coin	flour	kneel	parent	seventh	tabernacle
altar	collect(or)	forever	knowledge	pour	shepherd	temple
amaze	confuse	frost	lean	praise	sink	test
amen	cousin	glory	magician	pray(er)	sixth	thorn(y)
angel	covenant	grain	main	preach	slave	throne
baptize	crucify	hail	manger	priest	slingshot	thunder
belly	curtain	harp	manna	prison	smell	tomb
bless(ing)	deliver	holy	meaning	protect	sneaky	tongue
blind	disciple	horn	messenger	reward	soldier	towel
burn	divide	incense	metal	ribbon	soul	tower
calm	empty	inn	miracle	robe	spear	twinkle
chain	evil	invite	myrrh	root	spies	waist
chariot	faith	jail	nephew	royal	spit	wrap
choose	fancy	jewel	net	sailor	spread	wrist
chose	fifth	join	obey	sandals	statue	
Christian	flame	kingdom	olive	servant	stuck	

5

More Than Just a Coloring Book

More than just a fun coloring book, *Bible Story Color 'n' Learn* proclaims God's Word, written in a style easily understood by young learners. A word bank (page 5) lists new words to learn that are also spotlighted throughout the stories.

From Adam and Eve to John's glimpse into heaven, this book highlights major Bible stories such as Noah's ark and the birth of Jesus, as well as lesser-known stories, including Elijah's chariot of fire and Gideon's small but mighty army.

Reading stories, coloring pictures, and discussing new words are all features designed to encourage interaction between you and the children you love. Photocopying the front and back of each story gives teachers the opportunity to send illustrated stories home to parents to discuss and complete with their children.

We invite you to use these simply written, fun, and interesting Bible stories to educate the children in your life, encouraging them to love God's Word while exploring their artistic sides.

Note: The NIV translation of the Lord's Prayer appears on page 128. Teachers and parents who would rather teach another version may cover this with a substitute before making photocopies of this page. For additional information about the text of the stories, see page 2.

God Makes a Beautiful World

God Makes a Beautiful World

Genesis 1:1–23

In the beginning, there were no living things. There were no plants or animals. There was no land and no water. Nothing was in the sky. There was no sun. There was no moon. There were no stars. It was very dark and very quiet. Then, God made the heavens and the earth.

God said, "Let there be light." Light filled the sky, and God saw that it was good. That was the end of the first day.

For three days, God made the earth. He made land, oceans, and rivers. He made trees and flowers. He filled the sky with the sun, the moon, and the stars that twinkle at night.

God looked at everything, and He saw that it was good. But, God was not finished yet!

On the fifth day, God made the animals that live in the water and in the air. He made them in many sizes, shapes, and colors. God made the birds that fly in the sky. He made the fish and the animals that live in the water. When God looked around, He was very happy.

New Words to Learn!
fifth, twinkle

God Makes People

God Makes People

Genesis 1:24–31, 2:1–23, 3:20

On the sixth day, God made the animals that live on the land. But, He was still not finished. He wanted someone to take care of the earth. He wanted someone to enjoy what He had made. God said, "I will make a man."

God scooped dust from the ground. He shaped it into a man. Then, God breathed on the man. The man became alive.

God called the man Adam. God gave Adam a beautiful garden. God named it The Garden of Eden.

God did not want Adam to be alone in the garden. So, God made a woman. Adam named her Eve.

God looked at all that He had made. He saw the land and the water. He saw the plants and the animals. He saw Adam and Eve. He was very happy with this beautiful place. It was the seventh day. God was finished. He rested.

New Words to Learn!
alive, seventh, sixth

A Snake in the Garden

A Snake in the Garden

Genesis 2:16–17, 3:1–5

The Garden of Eden was a great place to live. Flowers grew everywhere. There were fruits and vegetables to eat. Adam and Eve did not get sick. They were never sad. They never got mad.

God was glad that Adam and Eve were His friends. He told them that they would always be happy.

God had one very important rule. He told Adam that he could eat the fruit from any of the trees except one. God said, "If you eat the fruit from the tree of knowledge, you will die." Adam told Eve about God's rule.

One day, a snake came into the garden. God made snakes smart and tricky. The snake asked Eve, "Did God tell you not to eat the fruit from any of these trees?"

Eve said, "There is only one tree that we should not eat from. If we touch or eat the fruit from that tree, we will die."

The snake told Eve a lie. "You will not die if you eat fruit from that tree," the snake said. "But, you will become as smart as God. That is why God does not want you to eat it."

Eve did not know if she should believe God or if she should believe the snake.

New Word to Learn!
knowledge

A Very Sad Day

A Very Sad Day

Genesis 3:6–23

Eve looked at the fruit from the tree of knowledge. It looked good. It was ready to eat.

Eve listened to the sneaky snake's lies. The snake told her not to listen to God. He told Eve that she would not die if she ate the fruit.

Eve picked the fruit from the tree. She bit into it. It was juicy and tasty.

Eve gave the fruit to Adam. He ate the fruit too. Adam and Eve knew that they had broken God's rule. They felt very sad.

Adam and Eve heard God walking in the garden. They hid behind some trees. God asked, "Where are you?" Adam told God that he was hiding because he was afraid.

God asked Adam if he and Eve had eaten the fruit from the tree of knowledge. Adam said sadly, "Yes."

Eve told God that the snake had tricked her. God was not happy. He told the snake, "You will crawl on your belly and eat dust every day of your life."

God told Adam and Eve, "You did not listen to me. Now you will not live forever. You will have to work hard every day for as long as you live."

Then, God made Adam and Eve leave the beautiful garden that He had made for them. It was a sad day in the Garden of Eden. Still, God loved Adam and Eve very much.

New Words to Learn!
belly, forever, knowledge, sneaky

Noah Builds an Ark

Noah Builds an Ark

Genesis 6–7

God looked at the people that He had made. He did not like what he saw. The people were mean to each other. They did bad things.

God was sad. He said, "I will flood the earth. Everything on the earth will die."

God was happy with one man. His name was Noah. Noah always obeyed God. So, God made a promise to Noah. God told Noah that He would save him and his family from the flood.

God told Noah to build a large boat called an ark. The ark would hold Noah's family. God told Noah to bring at least two of every animal into the ark.

Noah knew that he must do what God said. First, he built the ark. Next, he gathered food for his family and for the animals.

Mother and father animals of every kind came to Noah. He brought the animals inside the ark.

Noah and his family went into the ark. Then, God closed the door of the ark. Rain fell from heaven for 40 days and 40 nights. Everything on the earth died. God saved Noah and his family. Everything inside the ark was safe.

New Word to Learn!
obey

God Sends a Rainbow

God Sends a Rainbow

Genesis 7:19–24, 8–9

God made a great flood. Water covered the earth. It covered the mountains and the trees. It covered every living thing. The people and the animals in the ark were safe.

The ark stayed in the water for 150 days. Then, God sent a strong wind over the earth. The ark landed on top of a mountain.

Noah opened a window on the ark. He sent out a raven. The raven could not find dry land. Then, Noah sent out a dove. The dove could not find a dry place to put its feet.

Noah waited seven days. He sent out the dove again. The dove flew back with a fresh olive leaf in its beak. Noah knew that the water had gone down.

God told Noah, "It is time to leave the ark." Noah and his family came out of the ark. The animals came out too.

God made a promise to Noah. He said, "I will not flood the earth again. Even when people are bad, I will not destroy every living thing again."

God made a beautiful rainbow in the sky. God told Noah, "Every time a rainbow appears in the clouds, I will remember my promise. My promise will last forever."

New Words to Learn!
forever, olive

The Tower of Babel

The Tower of Babel

Genesis 11:1–9

Many years passed after the flood. People around the world all spoke the same language. The people gathered in one place. They found a nice place to live near a river.

The people said, "We will build a city here. We will make bricks out of mud and straw. We will build a tower. The tower will reach to the heavens. Everyone will see how important we are."

God did not like this plan. He looked at the city. He saw the tower that the people were building. He did not want them to act like God. He knew that there would be trouble.

So, God made the people speak different languages. They tried to talk to each other. But, they could not understand each other.

The people stopped building the city and the tower. Then, God moved the people to places all over the earth.

The city was called Babel because God mixed up the language of the world.

New Word to Learn!

tower

The Land of Abram

Bible Story Color 'n' Learn • CD-204073

The Land of Abram

Genesis 12:1–10, 13, 15:2, 16:1, 18:11

Abram loved God. Abram had a wife named Sarai. Abram and Sarai were old. They did not have children. This made them sad.

One day, God spoke to Abram. God said, "You must leave your country. Leave your father's family. Go to a new place that I will show you."

God promised Abram, "I will bless you. You will be a blessing to others."

Abram listened to God. He took Sarai and his nephew Lot with him. They packed everything that they had. Abram and his family traveled for a long time. They stayed in many places.

Abram became rich. He had gold, silver, and many animals. His nephew Lot also had many animals. But soon, there was not enough food and water for all of the animals.

Abram told Lot, "We can share the land. You can pick the part that you want."

Lot was not fair to Abram. He picked the best land for himself.

After Lot moved to his land, God spoke to Abram. God said, "I will give you all of the land that you see. It will be for you and for your children."

Now, Abram and Sarai knew that they would have children. They built an altar to honor God.

New Words to Learn!
altar, bless(ing), nephew

God's Promise to Abram

God's Promise to Abram

Genesis 15:1–6, 17:1–18, 18:10–15, 21:1–6

God made a promise to Abram. God told Abram, "Look up at the sky. Count the stars, if you can. Your family will grow. There will be more children than there are stars in the sky." Abram believed God's words.

God changed Abram's name to Abraham, which means *father of many*. God changed Sarai's name to Sarah. God said, "She will be the mother of kings."

Abraham was 99 years old. God told Abraham, "This time next year, Sarah will have a son. You will name him Isaac."

Sarah heard what God said. She laughed to herself. Sarah thought that she was too old to have a baby.

God asked Abraham, "Why did Sarah laugh? Is there anything that is too hard for God? I will return to you in one year. Sarah will have a son."

God kept his promise to Abraham and Sarah. One year later, God gave them a son. Abraham and Sarah named him Isaac. His name means "laughing one."

Two Different Brothers

Two Different Brothers

Genesis 25:19–28, Genesis 28

Isaac and Rebekah had twin sons. They named their first son Esau. His body was covered with hair. They named their second son Jacob.

Esau and Jacob grew up. Esau was a good hunter. He liked to be outside. Jacob was quiet. He did not like to be outside. He stayed at home near the tents.

Esau was not nice to Jacob. He was mad at Jacob most of the time. Isaac and Rebekah were sad. They wanted to help Jacob.

Isaac told Jacob to go to his uncle's town. Isaac wanted Jacob to find a wife. Isaac said, "May God bless you and give you many children. When you come back, you can be in charge of this land."

Jacob listened to his father. He started on his trip. He prayed that God would keep him safe. He prayed that God would bless his life.

New Words to Learn!
bless, pray

A Stairway to Heaven

A Stairway to Heaven

Genesis 28:10–22

Jacob's uncle lived far away. The trip to his uncle's house took a long time. Jacob walked all day. He stopped to rest at night.

Jacob found a stone on the ground. He put it under his head and went to sleep.

Jacob had a dream. He saw stairs that went to heaven. Angels went up and down the stairs. Then, Jacob heard a voice. It was God!

God said, "I promise to give all of this land to you. You will have many children. They will live all over the earth."

God told Jacob, "I am with you. I will not leave you."

Jacob woke up. He said, "This must be the house of God. This is the gate of heaven!"

In the morning, Jacob picked up the stone that was under his head. He built an altar with it. He asked God to keep him safe. Jacob asked God to give him food to eat and clothes to wear.

Jacob promised, "You will be my God." Jacob left the stone altar to show this promise to God.

New Words to Learn!
altar, angel

Brothers and Friends

Brothers and Friends

Genesis 31:3, 31:17–18, 32:3–32, 33:1–4

Jacob lived with his uncle for a long time. God blessed Jacob with a wife and a large family. He gave Jacob many animals. After many years, God told Jacob, "Go back to your father's house. I will be with you."

Jacob was worried. He had not seen his brother Esau in many years. Jacob wondered if Esau still did not like him.

Jacob and his family traveled all day. They stopped to set up camp. Jacob sent men to talk to Esau. They told Esau that Jacob wanted to be friends.

The men came back. They told Jacob, "Your brother is coming to meet you. He has 400 men with him!" Jacob was afraid, so he asked God for help.

Jacob sent gifts to Esau. He sent goats, camels, cows, bulls, and donkeys. Jacob also sent his family ahead of him.

Jacob was alone that night. But, during the night, someone started fighting with Jacob. He fought with the man all night Finally, the man said, "Let me go. It is morning."

Jacob said, "I will not let you go until you bless me."

The man said, "I am changing your name to Israel. You fought with God and man, and you won!" Jacob knew that the man was God. He knew that God had let him live.

The next day, Jacob walked to Esau's house. When they saw each other, Jacob bowed to Esau. Esau ran to Jacob and hugged him. Jacob and Esau were friends! Jacob knew that God had been kind to him.

· ·

New Word to Learn!
bless

A New Coat and Big Dreams

31

A New Coat and Big Dreams

Genesis 35:18, 35:23–26, 37:1–11

Jacob had 12 sons. Joseph was the 11th son. When Joseph was 17 years old, his father made him a coat. It was a beautiful coat of many colors.

Joseph was proud of his coat. Joseph's brothers did not have fancy coats like Joseph's. His brothers were angry about the coat, so they were mean to him.

One night, Joseph had a dream. The dream was about Joseph and his brothers. They were working in a field. They were putting wheat into bunches. Joseph saw his bunch of wheat stand up. Then, his brothers' bunches of wheat bowed down to his.

Joseph was happy about his dream. He wondered what it meant. He told his brothers about the dream. His brothers asked, "Do you think that you will rule over us? Is that what the dream means?" They were not happy about Joseph's dream.

Joseph had another dream. In this dream, Joseph saw the sun, the moon, and 11 stars. They were all bowing to Joseph.

Joseph told his father about the dream. His father asked, "Will your mother, your brothers, and I bow in front of you one day?" No one knew what these dreams meant.

Joseph Helps His Brothers

Joseph Helps His Brothers

Genesis 37:12, 37:31–33, 41:25–41, 42–43, 45–46, 47:11–12, 50:20

One day, Joseph was watching the flocks. He did not come home. Joseph's father Jacob thought that a wild animal had killed Joseph. For a long time, Jacob thought that Joseph was dead. But, Joseph was not dead. He was one of the king's officers. He lived in the king's palace in Egypt.

The king had a dream. God helped Joseph understand the dream. Joseph told the king what the dream meant. He told the king that soon people would not have enough food.

The king listened to Joseph. He saved food for his people. People everywhere were hungry. But, Egypt had a lot of food. The people of Egypt shared their food with others.

Ten of Jacob's sons went to Egypt to buy food. Benjamin, the youngest, stayed home. The brothers went into Joseph's house. They bowed to him. They did not know that he was Joseph. He remembered the dreams that he had as a child. He had dreamed that his brothers bowed to him. The dreams had come true!

Joseph gave his brothers sacks of food. He said, "One brother must stay until you bring me Benjamin." The brothers came back with Benjamin. Then, Joseph told his brothers who he was.

Joseph's brothers were afraid. They had been mean to Joseph when he was young. Joseph said, "Do not be afraid. You did something bad, but God turned it into something good. God sent me here to save lives."

Joseph asked for his father and brothers to join him. The family was together in Egypt.

A Baby in a Basket

A Baby in a Basket

Exodus 1, 2:1–5

God kept his promise to Jacob. Jacob had many children. His children grew up. They had many children. They lived all over the earth. They were the Israelites.

The king of Egypt was worried. He thought that the Israelites were too powerful. The king told his soldiers to make the Israelites slaves. The king treated the Israelites badly. He made them work very hard.

Israelite families grew. So, the king gave another order. He told his men that every Israelite baby boy must die.

One mother made a plan to save her son. She hid him from the king's soldiers. She put her son in a basket. She covered the basket. Then, she placed the basket in the tall grass of the Nile River.

The baby had a big sister. Her name was Miriam. She stayed close to her baby brother and watched. The king's daughter went to the river to take a bath. She walked near the tall grass. She saw the covered basket.

New Words to Learn!

slave, soldier

His Name Is Moses

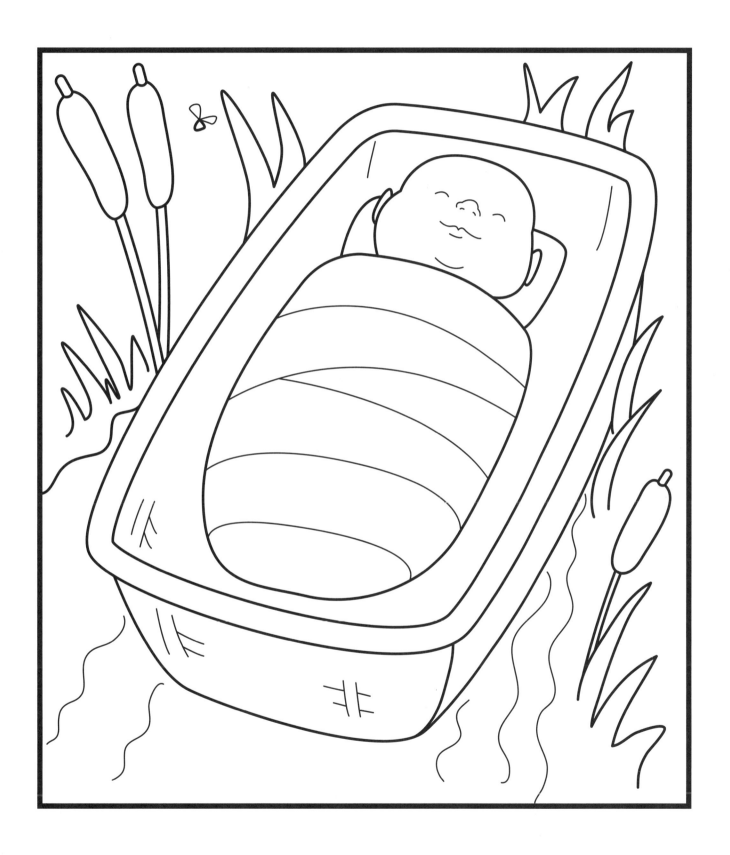

37

His Name Is Moses

Exodus 2:5–10

The king's daughter lived in the royal palace. She was a princess. One day, she went to the Nile River to take a bath. She saw a basket in the tall grass. She wondered what was in it.

The princess uncovered the basket. She saw a baby. The baby started crying, so she picked him up.

The princess knew that her father was angry at the Israelites. She knew that Israelite baby boys were in danger. The princess said, "This must be an Israelite baby."

The baby's big sister Miriam was hiding close by. She and her mother had put the baby there to keep him safe from the king's soldiers.

Miriam walked up to the princess. Miriam asked her, "Should I find someone to take care of this baby?"

The princess said, "Yes."

Miriam came back with her own mother. The princess said, "Take care of this baby until he is older. Then, bring him back to me."

The baby's mother was happy to take care of him. She took the baby back to the princess when he was older. The princess said, "I will name him Moses because I lifted him out of the water."

New Word to Learn!
royal

The Burning Bush

The Burning Bush

Exodus 3:1–12

When Moses grew up, the Israelites were still slaves. The new king made them work hard in Egypt. God was sad. He wanted to help the Israelites.

Moses left the palace where he lived. He became a shepherd. One day, he took a flock of sheep to a mountain. He saw a bush that was on fire. The bush was covered in flames, but it was not burned. Moses walked close to the bush. A voice said his name.

"Moses! Moses!" the voice of God said.

Moses answered, "Here I am."

God told Moses, "I am the God of your father, the God of Abraham, Isaac, and Jacob. Take off your sandals. This is holy ground."

Moses took off his sandals. He hid his face. He was afraid to look at God.

God said, "I have come to save my people. I have heard them crying. Tell the king to let My people go. You will lead them to a better place."

Moses did not think that he could do what God said. He did not think that the king would listen to him.

God told him, "I will be with you. Everyone will know that I have sent you. You will bring My people out of Egypt. All of you will pray to Me on this mountain."

. . . .

New Words to Learn!

flame, holy, pray, sandals, shepherd, slave

Moses the Messenger

Moses the Messenger

Exodus 4:27, 5, 6:1

God told Moses to go to Egypt to talk to the king. Moses did what God said. Moses took his brother Aaron with him.

Moses said to the king, "God says you must let His people go."

The king said, "Who is this God? I do not know Him. Why should I listen to Him? I will not let the people go."

Moses said, "If you do not let the Israelites go, God will bring bad things to Egypt."

The king did not care. He said that he would not let the people go. The king made God's people work even harder. The king would not give them the supplies that they needed to do their jobs.

The Israelites were angry with Moses and Aaron. The Israelites blamed the brothers for their problems.

Moses was sad. He asked God, "Did you send me to make life harder for Your people? You promised to save them. Now they have more trouble."

God spoke to Moses. He said, "Watch what I do to the king. He will see My power. Then, he will let the Israelites go."

New Word to Learn!
messenger

Frogs, Bugs, Hail, and More!

Frogs, Bugs, Hail, and More!

Exodus 7:1–13, 8–11:1

The king of Egypt did not believe in God's power. He would not let the Israelites go.

God gave Moses and Aaron special power. God told them to go to the king. He told Aaron to throw down his walking stick. The stick turned into a snake. The king was surprised. But, he did not change his mind. He would not let the Israelites go.

Moses and Aaron went to the king many times. One time, Aaron raised his walking stick over the land. God covered the land with frogs. The king said to Moses, "I will let the people go if you get rid of the frogs." Moses prayed to God. He asked God to get rid of the frogs. But, the king would not let the people go.

God sent many biting flies. Later, he sent many more flies. The king still said, "No! I will not let the people go."

God made more bad things happen to the king and his people. First, the farm animals got sick. Next, dust fell from the sky. The dust landed on the people. The dust made sores on the people's skin. But, the king did not change his mind.

God told Moses to lift his hand to the sky. It rained, hailed, and thundered. The storm destroyed the land. Next, God covered the land with bugs. The bugs ate all of the plants that were left.

Then, God made the sky dark for three days. Still, the king would not let the Israelites go. God told Moses, "I will do one more thing to the king and to Egypt. Then, he will let you and your people go."

New Words to Learn!
hail, pray, thunder

The King Changes His Mind

The King Changes His Mind

Exodus 11, 12:12–37

God told Moses to give the king one more chance. He said, "Tell the king to let God's people go. If the king does not listen, the oldest child and the oldest animal in every family will die. Even the king's own son will die."

The king did not change his mind. He still said, "No!"

God told Moses to talk to every Israelite family. God wanted to keep their oldest children safe.

Moses told the Israelites what God had said. Moses said, "Mark the tops and sides of your doors. Tonight, God will search for the marks. He will see the marks and know that you are His people. He will pass over your houses. He will not hurt the people inside."

In the middle of the night, the Egyptians cried. Someone had died in every Egyptian family.

The king called for Moses. He said to Moses, "Get out of here! You and all of the Israelites, leave my people! Take your flocks and herds with you."

The king said to Moses, "Give me your blessing."

God made the Egyptians kinder. The Egyptians gave gold, silver, and clothes to the Israelites. Then, God led Moses and the Israelites out of Egypt.

New Word to Learn!
blessing

A Cloud and Fire Lead the Way

47

A Cloud and Fire Lead the Way

Exodus 13:17–22; 14:1–20

God helped Moses and the Israelites leave Egypt. God appeared to them in a cloud. The cloud looked like a tall post. By day, the post stayed ahead of the people. It showed them the way.

At night, God gave the Israelites a light to show them where to go. The light looked like a tall post of fire. The cloud helped the people travel in the day. The fire helped the people travel at night.

The king of Egypt was mad that he had let the Israelites go. He said to his army, "What have we done? We have let the Israelites go. Now we have no one to do our work!"

The king took his army and his chariots to find the Israelites. He planned to take the Israelites back to Egypt.

The Israelites camped near the Red Sea. They saw the king's army coming with horses and chariots. The Israelites were scared. They asked God to help them.

The Israelites asked Moses, "Why did you bring us here to die? We wish we were still slaves in Egypt."

Moses said, "Do not be afraid. God will save us. He will fight for us."

That night, the tall post of cloud came. This time, it stopped between the king's army and the Israelites. The king's army could not see the Israelites in the dark. So, the Israelites were safe all night.

New Words to Learn!
chariot, slave

A Path Through the Sea

A Path Through the Sea

Exodus 14:15–31

The Israelites camped near the Red Sea. The Egyptian army was nearby with horses and chariots. They were ready to fight the Israelites. The Egyptian army wanted to take the Israelites back to Egypt.

But, the Egyptian army could not see the Israelites. God had appeared in front of them like a tall cloud. The army did not go near the Israelites that night.

God spoke to Moses. He said, "Why are the people of Israel crying out to me? Tell them to keep moving. Hold out your walking stick. Reach out your hand over the sea. I will make a path through the sea. Then, the people can cross on dry land."

Moses did what God said. God made a path through the sea! The Israelites began walking across dry land. There was a wall of water on each side of them.

The Egyptian army got onto their horses and chariots. They followed the Israelites into the sea. The Egyptian army moved slowly because God made the wheels of the chariots fall off.

The last Israelite crossed the Red Sea. Then, God told Moses to raise his hand over the water again. Moses did what God said.

The water covered the dry land. The water covered the Egyptians. God had saved the Israelites.

The Israelites praised God for His help. They trusted God. They also trusted Moses.

. . . .

New Words to Learn!

chariot, praise

Bread from Heaven

Bread from Heaven

Exodus 15:22–27, 16:1–30

Moses and the Israelites walked for a long time in the desert. It was hot and dry. They were very thirsty. They came to a place with water. They tasted it. It tasted bad.

God told Moses to throw a piece of wood into the water. Moses did what God said. The water became sweet. The people had water to drink. They were happy.

Soon, the people were unhappy again. "We have no food. We are hungry. We should have stayed in Egypt. We had food there."

God heard His people's cries. He told Moses, "I will send the people bread from heaven. The people will know that I am taking care of them."

The next morning, the people saw thin flakes everywhere. It looked like frost on the ground. Moses said that it was bread sent by God. The people called the bread *manna*.

Moses told the people, "God will send manna every morning. Take what you need. Eat all of the bread that you take. Do not save any for the next day. On the sixth day, gather enough to eat for two days.

Each day, God sent manna. Most people took what they needed. On the sixth day, they gathered enough for two days. On the seventh day, they rested.

New Words to Learn!
frost, manna, seventh, sixth

Water from a Rock

Water from a Rock

Exodus 17:1–6

The Israelites were traveling across the desert. They stopped to set up camp. They could not find water near the camp.

The people were mad. They told Moses that they were thirsty. They said, "Give us water to drink!"

Moses said, "Why do you yell at me? Why do you want to test God?"

The people were angry with Moses. They asked him, "Why did you bring us out of Egypt? We will die without water. Our animals will die too."

Moses asked God what he should do. God said, "Carry your walking stick. Take a few men with you. Walk ahead of the men. When you reach the large rock, I will be there. Hit the rock with your stick."

The men watched Moses walk to the rock. They saw him hit it with his stick. Water came out of the rock. There was enough water for every person and animal to drink.

New Word to Learn!
test

The Ten Commandments

The Ten Commandments

Exodus 19, 20:1–17, 32:15–16

The Israelites traveled for three months. They came to a large mountain. God said to Moses, "Tell the people to meet Me here in three days."

God said, "Tell My people that they are special to Me. That is why I led them out of Egypt. But, they must follow My rules."

Moses gathered the people at the bottom of the mountain. The mountain shook. The people heard a trumpet. They saw smoke come from the mountain. God told Moses to climb the mountain.

Moses went to the top of the mountain. God told Moses His rules. He called them the Ten Commandments. Later, God wrote the commandments on flat pieces of stone.

Moses carried the stones down the mountain. Then, he shared God's rules with the Israelites. Moses told the people, "God has promised that He will help us. But, we must follow His rules."

Moses read the Ten Commandments to the people.

1. Love God more than you love anyone else.
2. Don't make anything in your life more important than God.
3. Always say God's name with love and respect.
4. Honor the Lord by resting on Sunday.
5. Love and respect your mom and dad.
6. Never hurt anyone.
7. Always be true to your husband or wife.
8. Don't take anything that isn't yours.
9. Always tell the truth.
10. Be happy with what you have. Don't wish for other people's things.

God's Covenant

God's Covenant

Exodus 32:30, 34, 35:22–29, 37:1–9, 40:34–38; Numbers 10:33–34

The Israelites did not follow God's rules. They broke the Ten Commandments. God appeared in a cloud. He told Moses to cut out two new stones. God wanted to write His commandments again.

God told Moses, "I do not get angry quickly. I am full of love. I forgive everyone who makes mistakes." God made a new promise to His people. Moses wrote the words on the new stones.

God spoke to Moses again. God wanted the people to build a holy tent. He called the tent a tabernacle. The people could pray to God in the tent.

Moses told the people, "This is what God wants you to do. You should do your work in six days and rest on the seventh day."

The Israelites used gold, silver, and jewels to make God's tent beautiful. Some workers made tables and altars. Other workers used red, purple, and blue yarn to make curtains.

God wanted a special box to hold His promises. The box is called the ark of the covenant. A covenant is a promise.

A worker made the box from wood. He made a gold angel for each end. He made two poles to carry the box.

The people finished the work. They began traveling again.

Each day, God came in a cloud over the tent. When the cloud went away, the people kept going.

At night, God sent a tall post of fire. It guarded the people when they rested. The cloud stayed with the Israelites everywhere that they traveled.

New Words to Learn!
altar, angel, covenant, curtain, holy, jewel, pray, seventh, tabernacle

The Land of Milk and Honey

The Land of Milk and Honey

Numbers 13, 14:1–9, 14:30

The Israelites walked for many days. They came to the land that God had promised them. They set up a camp.

God told Moses to send 12 leaders to see the land. They looked at the soil, trees, plants, and fruit. They studied the people, cities, and towns. They picked fruit and put it on a long pole. After 40 days, they came back to the camp. Two leaders carried the fruit on a pole between them.

The leaders told Moses, "We looked at the land. The soil grows many fruits and vegetables. It is the land of milk and honey. But, the people who live there are powerful. The cities are large. There are high walls around the cities."

Some leaders were afraid. They did not think that God would help them take over the land. These leaders told stories that were not true.

They said, "The land is not good. The people there are very tall. We look like grasshoppers next to them." God told Moses that He would not let these men come into the land of milk and honey.

Joshua and Caleb were two of the leaders. They believed that God would help them. They said, "We are not afraid. Those people are strong. But, God is stronger. God is with us."

God blessed Joshua, Caleb, and their children. God brought them into the land of milk and honey.

New Word to Learn!
bless

Rahab Helps God's People

Rahab Helps God's People

Joshua 1:1–2, 2:1–23

Moses led the Israelites to the land that God had promised them. But, Moses died before he could enter. God told Joshua to lead the Israelites into the promised land.

Joshua wanted to learn more about the land. He wanted to know more about the city of Jericho. So, Joshua sent two spies to Jericho.

The king knew that the spies were in Jericho. He heard that they were hiding at a woman's house. The woman's name was Rahab. The king sent his men to Rahab's house.

Rahab knew that God had promised the land to the Israelites. She knew that God had dried up the Red Sea for them. Rahab helped Joshua's spies hide. The king's men could not find them.

Rahab told Joshua's spies, "I know that your God is powerful. I have been kind to you. When your army takes over Jericho, will you be kind to my family?"

The spies said, "Yes. Bring your family inside your house. Then, hang a red rope from your window. Our army will see the rope. They will know that you are God's friend."

The spies left Rahab's house. They stayed in the hills for three days. The king's men stopped looking for them. The spies went back to Joshua. They told him what had happened.

New Word to Learn!
spies

The Walls of Jericho Fall

The Walls of Jericho Fall

Joshua 6

The people of Jericho knew that Joshua and the Israelites were coming. They closed the gates of Jericho. They knew that Joshua and the Israelites wanted to take over the city.

Joshua was near Jericho. God said to Joshua, "I am giving Jericho to you. I will give its king and his army to you too."

God told Joshua His plan to win Jericho. God said to Joshua, "Each day march once around the city with your men. Do this for six days. Carry the ark of the covenant with you"

Then, God said, "Seven priests should walk with you and blow trumpets. On the seventh day, the army and the priests should march around the city seven times. Then, the priests should blow their trumpets. Tell the army to shout when they hear the trumpets. The walls of the city will fall. You will all go in."

Joshua told the plan to the Israelites. When they shouted on the seventh day, the walls of Jericho fell. The Israelites ran into Jericho. They took over the city.

Joshua and his spies kept their promise to be kind to Rahab and her family. She had believed in the power of God. She had helped Joshua by hiding his spies. God blessed Joshua.

New Words to Learn!
bless, covenant, priest, seventh, spies

Deborah's Army

Deborah's Army

Judges 4–5

God was not happy with the Israelites. They did not follow His rules. God let a mean king rule the Israelites. He ruled for 20 years. The Israelites prayed to God for help.

Deborah was a leader and a judge. She was an Israelite. God talked to Deborah. He asked her to help His people. God told Deborah His plan.

Deborah talked to a man named Barak. She told him, "God wants you to help the people of Israel. You must lead an army against the king."

Barak said, "I will go if you go with me." So, Deborah and Barak gathered 10,000 men.

The king had an even bigger army and 900 chariots. Still, Deborah was not afraid. She knew that God would help the Israelites win.

The battle started. Then, the earth shook. Rain fell. The king's chariots got stuck in the mud.

The Israelites made a circle around the chariots. The Israelites won the battle. Barak and Deborah sang a song to thank God for His help.

New Words to Learn!
chariot, pray, stuck

God Chooses a Boy

God Chooses a Boy

Judges 6:1–16, 7:1–7

The Israelites did not follow God's rules. They prayed to other gods. So, God sent mean people to rule the Israelites. The rulers took the Israelites' animals. They killed the fruits and vegetables growing on the Israelites' land.

The Israelites ran away from the mean rulers. They hid in caves. They prayed, "God, help us! We are hungry and afraid!"

God heard His people's prayers. God sent an angel to a boy. The boy's name was Gideon. The angel said to Gideon, "The Lord is with you."

God told Gideon, "You are strong. I am sending you. You will save Israel."

Gideon asked, "How can I save Israel? My family is small. I am the youngest child."

God said, "I will be with you."

Gideon listened to God. He gathered a large army. God said, "I do not need a big army. I want a small army. I want people to know that I saved them."

Gideon told the men what God had said. Gideon said, "You may leave if you are afraid." More than half of the men left.

God said, "There are still too many men. Take them to the stream to drink water. Keep the men who drink water from their hands. Send away the men who drink from the stream like dogs."

Only 300 men drank from their hands. God said to Gideon, "I will use these 300 men. I will save Israel."

. . . .

New Words to Learn!
angel, choose, pray

A Battle Without a Fight

A Battle Without a Fight

Judges 7:8–22

Gideon had 300 men in his army. God promised Gideon that his men would win the battle against their enemy.

God sent Gideon and his servant to look at the enemy's camp. Gideon saw hundreds and hundreds of men and camels.

Gideon went back to his army. He followed God's plan. Gideon put his 300 men into three groups. He gave each man a trumpet. Then, he gave each man a jar with a light in it. He told the men, "Watch me. Do exactly what I do."

Gideon took 100 men to the edge of the enemy's camp. Gideon and his men blew their trumpets and broke their jars. They yelled, "For the Lord and for Gideon!" The rest of Gideon's army did the same thing.

The enemy heard the noise. It sounded like Gideon's army was bigger than theirs. The enemy army was confused. They started to fight each other.

Gideon and his men watched the enemy run away. Gideon and the Israelites won the battle without fighting.

New Words to Learn!
confuse, servant

Young Samson Grows Strong

Young Samson Grows Strong

Judges 13–15

The Israelites did not obey God. So, God let the Philistines rule the Israelites. The Philistines were mean to the Israelites for 40 years.

God sent an angel to an Israelite woman. The angel said, "You will have a son. He will save God's people from the Philistines. Your son will be different from other children. Do not cut his hair. He will work for God in a special way."

The woman told her husband what the angel said. The baby was born. His parents named him Samson. They did not cut his hair. Samson grew much stronger than other men.

One day, Samson saw a Philistine woman. He wanted to marry her. Samson's parents were sad. They said, "Philistines are not God's people." Samson did not listen to his parents.

Samson went to the woman's town to talk to her. On his way, a roaring lion attacked Samson. God gave Samson great strength. Samson fought the lion with his hands. Samson won the fight.

Samson married the Philistine woman. She was not a good wife. She did many things against Samson and against God. But, God wanted things to happen that way. It was part of His plan to help the Israelites.

New Words to Learn!
angel, obey, parent

God Makes Samson Strong Again

God Makes Samson Strong Again

Judges 16:2–31

Samson led the Israelites for 20 years. The Philistines did not like Samson. He was stronger than other men. They did not know that Samson's long hair made him strong.

Samson knew a Philistine woman named Delilah. Samson told Delilah a secret. He told her that his long hair made him strong.

Delilah told the secret to the Philistines. They waited until Samson was sleeping. Then, they cut his hair.

When Samson woke up, he was not strong anymore. The Philistines took him away. They made him blind. They put heavy chains around him. Then, they locked him in prison. Samson's hair began to grow again.

Thousands of Philistines gathered for a party. The guards took Samson out of prison. The wanted to show him to the crowd.

A man led Samson out of prison because Samson could not see. Samson asked the man, "Will you let me stand near the posts of the temple?" The man led Samson to the posts.

Samson prayed, "God, please make me strong one more time." God answered his prayer.

Samson put one hand on each post. He pushed with all his strength. Samson pushed away the posts. The temple fell on Samson and on thousands of Philistines.

New Words to Learn!
blind, chain, pray, prayer, prison, temple

Friends for Life

Friends for Life

Ruth 1:1–19, 2:10–12, 4:13–17

There was not enough food in Israel. So, some Israelites moved to other places. Naomi and her husband moved their family to Moab.

Naomi's husband died. Naomi stayed in Moab with her two sons. Both sons married Moab women. The women were named Ruth and Orpah. Ten years later, Naomi's sons died.

Naomi heard that Israel had food again. She told Ruth and Orpah, "I am going home to Israel. You should go back to your mothers' homes. You can meet new husbands there."

Ruth and Orpah did not want to go. But, Naomi said that it was best for everyone. Orpah kissed Naomi good-bye.

Ruth would not leave Naomi. Ruth said, "Where you go, I will go. Where you stay, I will stay. Your people are my people, and your God is my God."

Naomi and Ruth went to Bethlehem together. The people welcomed Ruth because she was Naomi's friend.

God blessed Ruth for her kindness to Naomi. Ruth married and had a family. Ruth's grandson was named Jesse. He had a son named David. When David grew up, God chose him to be king.

New Word to Learn!
bless, chose

God Calls Samuel

God Calls Samuel

1 Samuel 3:1–10, 3:19–21

Eli was an old priest. He could not see well. He had a helper named Samuel. Samuel stayed with Eli in the temple at night.

One night, a voice called, "Samuel!" Samuel ran to Eli's room. Samuel said, "Here I am. You called me."

Eli said, "I did not call you. Go back and lie down."

Samuel heard the voice call "Samuel!" again. He got up from his bed. He went to Eli's room. Eli again told Samuel, "I did not call you. Go back and lie down."

Samuel did not know that God was calling him. Samuel heard his name again. He went to Eli's room.

Eli told Samuel what to do the next time that he heard the voice. Eli told Samuel to say, "Speak, Lord. I am listening."

Samuel did what Eli told him. After that night, God spoke to Samuel many more times.

God was with Samuel as he grew up. God helped Samuel know things before they happened. Everyone knew that Samuel was a man of God.

New Words to Learn!
priest, temple

The Boy King

The Boy King

1 Samuel 16:1–13

Samuel was a wise man. God told him how to help people, even kings.

God was ready to choose a new king for Israel. He told Samuel, "I am sending you to Bethlehem. I will choose one of Jesse's sons to be king."

Samuel had a ram's horn that he filled with oil. He used the oil to bless people. God told Samuel, "Bring your horn. Fill it with oil to bless the new king."

Samuel went to Bethlehem. Jesse brought one of his sons to meet Samuel.

God told Samuel, "I will not choose this son. I do not care how people look on the outside. I look at what is in their hearts."

Jesse brought six of his other sons to meet Samuel. God did not choose them either.

Samuel asked, "Do you have other sons?"

Jesse said, "Yes, I have one more. David is my youngest son. He is taking care of my sheep."

Samuel said, "Bring him to me."

David walked into the house. God spoke to Samuel. God said, "He is the one. He will be the next king of Israel."

Samuel blessed David with oil. God gave power to David.

New Words to Learn!
bless, choose, horn

David and Goliath

David and Goliath

1 Samuel 17

The Philistines wanted to fight the Israelites. The Israelites lined up for battle. A Philistine man stepped out. His name was Goliath. He was more than nine feet tall. He wore a metal suit. The Israelites were scared to fight the giant man.

Goliath shouted to the Israelites, "Choose a man to fight me. If he wins, we will be your servants. If I win, you will serve us."

Goliath shouted every day for 40 days. David heard him shouting. David told King Saul that he wanted to fight Goliath. King Saul said, "You are just a boy. You are too young to fight."

David told King Saul that he was a shepherd. Sometimes wild animals tried to hurt his sheep. David had to fight off lions and bears to save his sheep.

David knew that Samuel had blessed him with God's power. David told the king, "The Lord protected me when I fought wild animals. The Lord will protect me now."

"Go," said King Saul. "The Lord be with you." King Saul gave David a metal suit to wear. David tried to walk around in it, but it was too heavy. He gave it back to King Saul.

Then, David chose five stones from a stream. He put them into his bag. He held his slingshot in his hand. He walked toward Goliath.

Goliath laughed at how small David was. David told Goliath, "You have a long spear. But, I have God on my side."

David took a stone from his bag. He put the stone in the slingshot. He shot it at Goliath. Goliath fell to the ground. The Philistines ran away. David won the battle!

. . . .

New Words to Learn!

choose, chose, metal, protect, servant, shepherd, slingshot, spear

Elijah Helps a Family

83

Elijah Helps a Family

1 Kings 17:1–16, 17:24

God wanted to help the Israelites. He chose Elijah to help Him.

God told Elijah that soon there would be no water to drink. He told Elijah to live near a stream. Elijah drank the water there. Birds fed him each day. But, there was no rain. So, the stream dried up.

Then, God told Elijah, "Go to town. You will meet a woman. She will give you food."

Elijah saw the woman. She was gathering sticks. Elijah said, "Will you give me a piece of bread? Will you give me some water to drink?"

The woman told Elijah that she had only a little flour in a jar and a little oil in a jug. Soon, she and her son would have nothing to eat.

Elijah said, "Do not be afraid. Go home and make some bread for me and for your family. God will give you flour and oil until He brings rain again."

The woman went home. She made bread. She gave some to Elijah.

She and her son had bread every day. The jar of flour was never empty. The jug always had oil in it. God had kept His promise.

New Words to Learn!

chose, empty, flour

A Chariot of Fire

A Chariot of Fire

2 Kings 2:1–15

Elijah had a good friend named Elisha. Elisha loved and honored Elijah for many years. Elijah grew old. He was ready to go to heaven. God told Elijah that a strong wind would take him to heaven.

Elijah told Elisha, "You should stay here. God told me to go to the Jordan River."

But, Elisha wanted to walk with him. They reached the river. Fifty men were there. Elijah rolled up his coat. He hit the water with it. The water parted. It made a dry path. Elijah and Elisha walked across the river.

Elijah said to Elisha, "Tell me what I can do for you before I go to heaven."

Elisha wanted God to give him great power. Elijah said, "It is yours if you can see me going to heaven."

A chariot of fire and horses of fire came between the men. Elisha watched Elijah go to heaven in a strong wind.

Then, Elisha saw Elijah's coat on the ground. He picked it up. Elisha went back to the river. He hit the water with Elijah's coat.

The water parted. Elisha walked across the river on dry ground. The fifty men watched. They said, "God has blessed Elisha with Elijah's spirit."

New Words to Learn!
bless, chariot

Elisha Helps a Man

Elisha Helps a Man

2 Kings 5:1–19

Naaman was a leader in King Aram's army. God helped Naaman win battles. Naaman was a brave man, but he had sores on his skin. King Aram wrote a letter to the king of Israel. He asked the king to make Naaman well.

The king read the letter. He became angry. He said, "I am not God! I cannot make people well!"

Elisha heard about Naaman. He sent a messenger to Naaman. The messenger told Naaman to come to Elisha's house. Naaman went to see Elisha. A man opened the door. The man told Naaman, "Elisha wants you to go to the Jordan River. Wash yourself seven times. Your skin will be well."

Naaman was angry. He thought that Elisha would come outside and pray for him. Naaman did not think that the Jordan River would make him well. He went away.

Naaman's friends said, "You should do what Elisha said. Wash yourself. Then, your skin will be well."

Naaman went to the Jordan River. He washed himself seven times. The sores were gone!

Naaman told Elisha, "Now I know that the God of Israel is real. Here is a gift for you."

Elisha would not take the gift. He said, "I serve the Lord. You can be sure that He lives. Go in peace."

New Words to Learn!

messenger, pray

Esther Saves Her People

Esther Saves Her People

Esther 2:1–7, 2:17, 3:1–6, 4–5, 7:1–7

When Esther was a little girl, her cousin took care of her. He was a Jewish man.

When Esther grew up, she married the king. He put a crown on Esther's head. He made her the queen.

The king had a helper named Haman. The king told everyone to kneel and pray to Haman. Esther's cousin would not kneel because he prayed only to God. This made Haman angry.

Haman planned to destroy all of the Jewish people in the kingdom. Esther's cousin told her, "Go to the king. Beg for safety for the Jewish people. We will pray."

Esther was afraid to ask the king to save her people. The king did not know that Esther was Jewish. Esther's cousin said, "Maybe God made you queen so that you could help your people."

Esther had a big feast for Haman and the king. After dinner, the king asked, "Esther, what can I do for you? I will give you anything that you wish."

Esther said, "My people and I will be destroyed. Will you please save us?"

"Who would let this happen?" the king asked.

"Haman," Esther answered. The king believed her. He stopped Haman's plan. Esther saved the Jewish people!

New Words to Learn!
kingdom, kneel, pray

The King's Dream

91

The King's Dream

Daniel 1:1–17, 2

Daniel and three of his friends were in the king's army. They followed God's rules.

God made Daniel and his friends smarter than most men. God helped Daniel understand the meanings of dreams.

The king had a dream. The dream worried him. He did not understand what his dream meant. He sent for wise men and magicians. They did not understand his dream.

The king was angry. He told Daniel to get rid of the wise men and magicians.

Daniel asked his friends to pray for God's help. God showed Daniel the meaning of the king's dream. Daniel went to tell the king.

Daniel told the king, "God showed me a statue in your dream. It had a gold head and silver arms."

Daniel told the king that God would give him great power. Three more kings would rule after him. Then, God would make a new kingdom. It would last forever.

The king said to Daniel, "You have explained my dream. Your God is the God of gods. He is the Lord of kings."

The king thanked Daniel. He asked Daniel and his friends to help him rule the kingdom.

New Words to Learn!
forever, kingdom, magician, meaning, pray, statue

Saved from the Fire

Saved from the Fire

Daniel 3

The king was worried about a dream he had. Daniel helped the king understand the dream. Then, the king asked Daniel and his friends to help him rule the kingdom.

The king built a statue like the one in his dream. He told the people to listen for a flute, harp, or horn. When they heard the music, they must bow and pray to the statue. If they did not pray to the statue, they would be thrown into a fire.

Daniel's friends would not bow to the statue. They told the king that they would pray only to God. The king was angry. He asked, "Will your God save you from the fire?"

"We are not afraid," the men said. "God will save us."

The king told his soldiers to make the fire hotter. He told the soldiers to tie the men with ropes and throw them into the fire. The soldiers obeyed the king.

The king looked into the fire. He jumped to his feet. He shouted to the soldiers, "You threw three men into the fire. Why do I see four men? One looks like an angel. They are not tied up. They are walking around. The fire is not hurting them!"

The king told the men to come out. They did not have burns on their bodies or clothes. They did not smell like smoke.

The king praised God for sending an angel to save the men from the fire. The king gave the men more power to help him rule the kingdom.

. . . .

New Words to Learn!

angel, burn, harp, horn, kingdom, obey, praise, pray, smell, soldier, statue

Daniel in the Lions' Den

Daniel in the Lions' Den

Daniel 6

Daniel helped the king rule the kingdom. The king trusted Daniel. He wanted to put Daniel in charge of the whole kingdom.

Some of the king's men did not want Daniel to be powerful. They planned to get rid of him. They said to the king, "You should make a new law. Tell the people that they must pray to you for 30 days. Put them into the lions' den if they pray to any gods." The king agreed.

The king's men went to Daniel's home. They saw him praying to God. When they told the king, he was sad. The king did not want to hurt Daniel. But, the law could not be changed.

The men took Daniel to the lions' den. The king said to Daniel, "You have always honored your God. I hope that He will save you."

The men put a large stone at the opening of the den. Daniel could not get out of the lions' den. The king was worried about Daniel. The king did not eat or sleep that night.

Early the next morning, the king went to the lions' den. The stone was still in place. The king called, "Daniel, did your God save you?"

Daniel said, "Yes, an angel closed the lions' mouths. They did not hurt me." The king was happy. He told his men to let Daniel out.

The king wrote a letter to the people of his kingdom. He wrote, "I command everyone to respect Daniel's God. He saved Daniel from the power of the lions. He is the living God. He will rule forever."

New Words to Learn!

angel, forever, kingdom, pray

Jonah and the Storm

Jonah and the Storm

Jonah 1:1–16

God wanted Jonah to talk to people who were doing bad things. He told Jonah to go to the city where the people lived. But, Jonah did not listen to God.

Jonah ran away from God. He got on a ship that was sailing to another place.

God sent a strong wind across the sea. The sailors on the ship were afraid. They thought that their ship would break. They threw things into the water to make the ship lighter. They prayed to their gods for help.

Jonah did not help the sailors. He did not pray to God. Jonah went to sleep. The captain asked Jonah, "How can you sleep? Ask your God to save us from this storm."

Jonah and the sailors knew why God had sent the storm. It was because Jonah had not listened to God. Jonah told the captain, "Throw me into the water, and the storm will stop." The sailors did not want to throw Jonah into the water.

They tried to row the ship back to land, but the storm got worse. The men were afraid that they would drown. They prayed to Jonah's God for forgiveness. They threw Jonah into the water.

The sea was peaceful again. When the sailors saw what happened, they believed in the power of Jonah's God.

New Words to Learn!

pray, sailor

Jonah and the Big Fish

Jonah and the Big Fish

Jonah 1–3

Jonah was on a ship. He was running away from God. A bad storm came. The ship was about to sink.

Jonah told the sailors on the ship, "Throw me into the sea and the storm will stop." The sailors did what Jonah said. The storm stopped.

Jonah sank to the bottom of the ocean. He almost drowned. God sent a large fish to swallow Jonah. Jonah was inside of the fish for three days.

Jonah prayed to God. He said, "I know that You are the one who saves. I will do whatever You want me to do. I promise."

God told the fish to spit out Jonah. He told the fish to put Jonah on dry land.

God told Jonah to go to a city where people were doing bad things. Jonah kept his promise to God.

Jonah went to the city. He told the people that they must change their ways. He told them that they should follow God.

Jonah said, "If you do not do what God says, He will destroy your city in 40 days."

The ruler of the city believed Jonah. The ruler told the people to change their bad ways. The people listened to the ruler. They prayed to God. God forgave them. God did not destroy their city.

New Words to Learn!
pray, sailor, sink, spit

Gabriel's Good News

Gabriel's Good News

Luke 1:26–56

Mary lived in Nazareth. Soon, she would marry Joseph. God sent an angel to visit Mary. The angel's name was Gabriel.

Gabriel told Mary, "The Lord is with you. He is very happy with you."

Mary was worried. She did not understand why the angel came to her.

Gabriel said, "Do not be afraid. You will have a son. You will name him Jesus. He will be the Son of God. He will rule forever."

"How can this be?" Mary asked Gabriel.

The angel said, "The Holy Spirit will make this happen. Anything is possible with God."

"I serve God," Mary said. "Let this happen to me."

Mary hurried to visit her cousin Elizabeth. Mary knew that Elizabeth was going to have a baby too.

God told Elizabeth that Mary had special news. Elizabeth heard Mary coming.

Elizabeth said, "You are blessed among all women. Your child is blessed too. You will be the mother of my Lord!"

- -

New Words to Learn!
angel, bless, cousin, forever, holy

Jesus Is Born

Jesus Is Born

Luke 2:1–21

A powerful ruler wanted to count his people. Every man had to take his family to the town where he was born. Officers would count the people. Then, they could go home.

Joseph was born in Bethlehem. So, he and Mary went there to be counted. It was almost time for Mary's baby to be born.

Bethlehem was filled with people waiting to be counted. There was no place in the inn for Joseph and Mary to sleep.

Mary and Joseph found a place to stay. It was where animals slept. It had a manger to hold the animals' food. When the baby boy was born, Mary wrapped Him in cloths. She placed Him in the empty manger.

That night, shepherds were in the fields near Bethlehem. They were watching their flocks. An angel came to them. The shepherds were scared.

The angel said, "Do not be afraid. I have great news for you and for all people. A baby has been born. He will save the world! You can find Him in Bethlehem. He is lying in a manger."

More angels came. They said, "Glory to God in the highest. Peace on earth."

The shepherds went to Bethlehem. They saw Jesus lying in the manger. The shepherds told people the great news. The shepherds praised God for everything that had happened.

New Words to Learn!

angel, glory, inn, manger, praise, shepherd, wrap

Wise Men Follow a Star

Wise Men Follow a Star

Matthew 2:1–12

Jesus was born in Bethlehem. Far away, Wise Men watched the sky. They studied the stars. They saw a special star. They followed it to a city near Bethlehem.

The Wise Men talked to the people in the city. The Wise Men asked, "Where is the child who is the King of the Jews? We saw His star. We have come to honor Him."

Herod was the king. He heard about the Wise Men. He knew that they were looking for Jesus.

King Herod did not want Jesus to be king. King Herod secretly called for the Wise Men. The Wise Men went to King Herod.

King Herod told the Wise Men, "Look for the child in Bethlehem. Find Him, and tell me where He is. I want to honor Him too." But, King Herod was not telling the Wise Men the truth. King Herod wanted to get rid of Jesus.

The Wise Men followed the star to Bethlehem. The star stopped over the house where Jesus was.

When they arrived at the house, the Wise Men saw the child with His mother Mary. The Wise Men were filled with joy. They bowed to Jesus. They gave Him gifts of gold, incense, and myrrh.

Later, the Wise Men shared the same dream. The dream told them not to go back to King Herod. The Wise Men did what the dream said. They did not tell King Herod where Jesus was. They went home another way.

New Words to Learn!

incense, myrrh

Joseph's Dreams

Bible Story Color 'n' Learn • CD-204073

Joseph's Dreams

Matthew 2:13–23

Joseph had a dream. An angel told him to take Jesus and Mary to Egypt.

The angel said, "Jesus is not safe in Israel. King Herod wants to get rid of Him. Stay in Egypt. I will tell you when to leave." Joseph took Mary and Jesus to Egypt.

King Herod sent his men to Bethlehem. They looked for Jesus. They could not find Him. King Herod was angry for a long time.

Joseph and his family stayed in Egypt until King Herod died. Joseph had another dream.

An angel told Joseph, "Get up! It is safe in Israel now. Take Jesus and Mary back."

Joseph woke up his family. They left Egypt. They traveled until they were near Bethlehem.

Joseph heard about the new king. The new king was King Herod's son! Joseph was afraid that the new king would also want to get rid of Jesus.

Joseph had another dream. The dream told Joseph to go to a safer place. Joseph, Mary, and Jesus went to live in Nazareth.

New Word to Learn!
angel

Where Is Jesus?

Where Is Jesus?

Luke 2:41–52

Mary, Joseph, and Jesus went to Jerusalem. They shared the Passover Feast with their family and friends. Jesus was 12 years old.

The Passover Feast ended. People were traveling home. Mary and Joseph were with a group going to Nazareth. They thought that Jesus was in the group.

At the end of the day, Mary and Joseph could not find Jesus. They looked among their friends. They looked among the other families. No one had seen Jesus.

Mary and Joseph hurried back to Jerusalem. They looked for Jesus. Three days later, they found Him.

Jesus was sitting in a garden outside of the temple. He was listening to some teachers. He was asking questions. The teachers were surprised by Jesus' answers. They could not believe that a 12-year-old boy knew so much.

Mary said to Jesus, "We have been looking everywhere for You. We were worried!"

Jesus asked, "Why were you looking for Me? Didn't you know that I would be in My Father's house?" Jesus meant that the temple was God's house.

The family went home to Nazareth. Jesus grew stronger and wiser. God was happy with Jesus.

New Word to Learn!

temple

John the Baptist

Bible Story Color 'n' Learn • CD-204073

John the Baptist

Luke 1:57–60, 3:2–16; Mark 1:4–8

Elizabeth had a baby. She named him John.

When John grew up, he lived in the desert. He wore clothes made from camel hair. He ate bugs and wild honey.

God had a special job for John. God wanted John to tell people that Jesus was coming soon.

John traveled to many places around the Jordan River. He told people to stop doing bad things. He said that God would forgive them for their mistakes.

The people wanted God to be happy with them. They asked John, "What should we do?"

John gave the people rules to follow. He said, "Be happy with what you have. Share with others. Do not take things from others. Do not say bad things about people."

John baptized people in the river. He told the people to be ready for Jesus. He said that Jesus was coming soon.

John said to the people, "I baptize you with water. But, someone more powerful than I am will come. He will baptize you with God's Holy Spirit."

New Words to Learn!

baptize, holy

John Baptizes Jesus

Bible Story Color 'n' Learn • CD-204073

John Baptizes Jesus

John 1:19–34; Luke 3:21–22; Matthew 3:5–17

John the Baptist was at the Jordan River. He was telling people about God. He was baptizing people in the river.

Some men asked John the Baptist, "Are you Jesus? Are you the one who will save us?"

John said that he was not Jesus. John said, "Jesus is more powerful than I am. He will baptize you with the Holy Spirit."

Then, Jesus came to the river. John said to the people, "Look! Here is the man I told you about. He will take away the sins of the world. He is the Son of God."

Jesus asked John to baptize Him. John did not feel important enough to baptize Jesus.

Jesus told John, "It is right for you to do this." John baptized Jesus in the river.

Jesus prayed. A dove flew from heaven. It landed on Jesus.

A voice from heaven said to Jesus, "You are My Son. I love you. I am pleased with You."

New Words to Learn!

baptize, holy, pray

The Devil Tries to Trick Jesus

The Devil Tries to Trick Jesus

Luke 4:1–13; Mark 1:12–13

John baptized Jesus in the Jordan River. Then, God's Holy Spirit led Jesus to the desert.

Wild animals were in the desert, but they did not hurt Jesus. Angels kept Jesus safe from the animals.

Jesus was hungry. He had not eaten for 40 days.

The devil tried to trick Jesus. The devil said, "If You are the Son of God, turn this rock into bread."

Jesus knew that the devil was trying to make Him do something wrong. Jesus said to the devil, "Man does not live only on bread."

The devil tried to trick Jesus again. He led Jesus to a high place. He showed Jesus every kingdom in the world. The devil said, "I will give You the world if You will pray to me."

Jesus told the devil, "God is the only One that I pray to."

The devil tried again to trick Jesus. He led Jesus to Jerusalem. He told Jesus to stand on the highest point of the temple. The devil said, "Jump down from here. If You are the Son of God, angels will save You."

Jesus did not jump. Jesus told the devil, "God has told us not to test His power."

The devil left. He could not trick Jesus. The devil planned to try another time.

. . . .

New Words to Learn!

angel, baptize, holy, kingdom, pray, temple, test

Lots and Lots of Fish

Lots and Lots of Fish

Luke 5:1–11; Matthew 4:18–20

Jesus stood near the sea. He was talking about God to a large crowd. Jesus saw two fishing boats on the shore. The fishermen were washing their nets.

Jesus went onto Peter's boat. Jesus asked Peter to row away from the shore.

Jesus sat on the boat. He talked to the people on the shore.

Then, Jesus told Peter to row into deeper water. Jesus said, "Let down the nets."

Peter said, "We worked hard all night. We did not catch any fish. But, I will listen to You. I will let down the nets."

Peter dropped the nets into the water. The nets filled with fish. The nets were heavy. They started to break.

Fishermen on the other boat came to help. They filled the boats with fish. Both boats began to sink.

Peter and his friends were amazed. Jesus said to them, "Soon, you will catch people, not fish."

They knew that Jesus was giving them a new job. He wanted them to teach people about God.

Peter and his friends left everything that they had. They followed Jesus. They were Jesus' first disciples.

New Words to Learn!

amaze, disciple, net, sink

Water Turns into Wine

Water Turns into Wine

John 2:1–11

Jesus chose a few men to be his disciples. They helped Jesus teach people about God.

Jesus and his mother Mary went to a wedding. The disciples went too. There was a party after the wedding.

At the party, Mary told Jesus, "There is no more wine." Mary knew that Jesus could help.

Mary told the servants, "Do what Jesus tells you."

Jesus saw six jars. Each jar could hold many gallons of water.

Jesus told the servants, "Fill those jars with water." The servants filled each jar.

Jesus said, "Pour some into a cup. Give it to the man in charge of the dinner." The servants did what Jesus told them.

The man drank from the cup. It was wine! The servants knew that Jesus had turned the water into wine.

This was Jesus' first miracle. When the disciples saw this miracle, they put their faith in Jesus.

New Words to Learn!
chose, disciple, faith, miracle, pour, servant

A Hole in the Roof

121

A Hole in the Roof

Mark 2:1–12

Jesus was teaching inside a crowded place. There was no room to sit or stand. Some people stood outside to listen to Jesus.

Four men came to see Jesus. They wanted Jesus to help their friend. He could not walk.

The men carried their friend on a mat. The mat would not fit through the door.

So, the men climbed to the roof. They made a hole in the roof. They lowered the mat through the roof.

Jesus saw the man on the mat. He said to the man, "Son, your sins are forgiven."

Some men heard what Jesus said. They thought, "Jesus cannot forgive sins. He is not God."

Jesus knew what the men were thinking. Jesus told them, "The Son of Man can forgive sins."

Jesus said to the man on the mat, "Get up. Take your mat and go home."

Everyone was amazed to see the man stand up and walk. They praised God and said, "We have never seen anything like this!"

New Word to Learn!
amaze, praise

The Story of the Farmer

Bible Story Color 'n' Learn • CD-204073

The Story of the Farmer

Mark 4:1–20

Many people gathered by a lake to hear Jesus teach. A boat was at the shore. Jesus sat in the boat and told the people a story.

Jesus said, "A farmer went to plant his grain. He spread the seeds on the ground. Some seeds fell on a path. Birds ate every seed on the path.

"Some seeds fell on rocky places. The seeds began to grow. But, the plants did not grow roots. The plants died.

"Other seeds fell into thorny plants. The thorny plants filled the ground. There was no room for the seeds to grow.

"Some seeds fell on good soil. They grew into tall, strong plants. The farmer gathered 100 times more grain than he had planted."

Jesus' disciples listened to the story too. They wondered why Jesus would tell a story about a farmer.

Jesus told the disciples the meaning of the story. He said, "The farmer spreads his seeds like God spreads His Word. Some people hear God's Word. But, the devil comes to them. He takes away God's Word like the birds took away the seeds."

Then, Jesus said, "Some people hear God's Word with joy. But, they lose their faith when trouble comes. Their faith dies like the seeds on the rocks. Other people lose their faith when they want things that they cannot have. Their faith is like the seeds on thorny plants. It cannot grow."

Jesus told the disciples, "Keep your faith and watch it grow. It will grow like the seeds on good soil."

. . . .

New Words to Learn!

disciple, faith, grain, meaning, root, spread, thorny

Jesus Helps a Woman

Jesus Helps a Woman

Mark 5:22–34

Jesus was going to a man's house. A large crowd was following Him. Along the way, a woman joined the crowd. She had heard that Jesus could make people well.

The woman had been sick for 12 years. Every year she got worse. She wanted Jesus to help her. She said, "If I touch His clothes, I will be well."

The woman moved through the crowd. She got close to Jesus. She touched His clothes. Suddenly, she felt better. Her body was well.

Jesus felt some of His power leave Him when the woman touched His clothes. Jesus asked, "Who touched My clothes?"

Many people were crowding around Jesus. The disciples were surprised that Jesus could feel such a soft touch.

The woman was afraid. She did not want to tell Jesus that she had touched His clothes.

The woman kneeled in front of Jesus. She told Him the truth.

Jesus said, "Daughter, go in peace. You are free from your sickness. You are well because you had faith."

New Words to Learn!
disciple, faith, join, kneel

Jesus Teaches the Lord's Prayer

Jesus Teaches the Lord's Prayer

Matthew 4:23–25, 5:1–2, 6:5–15

People followed Jesus everywhere that He went. They heard that Jesus could help sick people.

One day, many people gathered to hear Jesus teach. Jesus went up on the side of a mountain to speak. The disciples were with Him.

Jesus told the people how to pray. He said, "When you pray, go into your room. Close the door. Pray to God. You cannot see Him. But, God will see what you did in secret. He will answer your prayer."

Jesus said that people should forgive anyone who sins against them. He said that God will forgive people's mistakes if they forgive each other.

Jesus gave the people this prayer:

Our Father in heaven, hallowed be your name, Your kingdom come, Your will be done on earth as it is in heaven. Give us today our daily bread. Forgive us our debts, as we also have forgiven our debtors. And lead us not into temptation, but deliver us from the evil one.

New Words to Learn!
deliver, disciple, evil, kingdom, pray

Jesus Stops a Storm

129

Jesus Stops a Storm

Matthew 8:16, 8:23–27

One night, Jesus was with His disciples. They got into a boat on a lake. The night was peaceful.

When they left the shore, Jesus went to sleep. Suddenly, a terrible storm came.

The wind began to roar. Waves crashed over the sides of the boat. Jesus kept sleeping.

The disciples woke up Jesus. They begged Jesus to help them. The disciples said, "Please save us, or we will drown!"

Jesus said, "Your faith is so small. Why are you afraid?"

Jesus got up. He told the wind and the waves to stop. They became calm. The storm ended.

The disciples were amazed. They knew that Jesus' power had stopped the storm.

The disciples asked each other, "What kind of man is this? Even the winds and the waves listen to Him!"

New Words to Learn!
amazed, calm, disciple, faith

Dinner for 5,000

Dinner for 5,000

Mark 6:30–44; John 6:9; Matthew 14:21

Jesus and His disciples talked to a large crowd for many hours. The people were hungry. They had not eaten all day.

The disciples did not have any food to give the people. The disciples told Jesus, "The people are hungry. Please send them away so that they can buy something to eat."

Jesus answered, "They do not need to leave. Give them something to eat."

The disciples could not buy food for 5,000 men. They did not have enough money.

Jesus asked His disciples, "How much food is here? Go and see." The disciples did what Jesus said.

Andrew was a disciple. He told Jesus, "Here is a boy. He has five small loaves of bread and two small fish. It is not enough for 5,000 people."

Jesus told his disciples to ask the people to sit. Then, Jesus looked to heaven. He thanked God for the food.

Jesus broke the five loaves of bread and divided the two fish. He told the disciples to give the bread and fish to the people.

The 5,000 men ate all that they wanted. The women and children ate as much as they wanted too.

Jesus told the disciples to gather what was left. The disciples came back to Jesus with 12 baskets. The baskets were filled with bread and fish. It was a miracle!

New Words to Learn!
disciple, divide, miracle

Jesus Walks on Water

Jesus Walks on Water

Matthew 14:22–33

Jesus and His disciples stood near a lake. Jesus told the disciples to get into their boat. He told them to sail to the other side of the lake.

Jesus did not go with the disciples. He went up on the side of a mountain to pray. He prayed until late at night.

The disciples were in the boat far from land. They looked across the water. They saw someone coming to the boat. He was walking on the water!

The disciples were afraid. They cried, "It is a ghost!"

Jesus told them, "Do not be afraid. It is me."

Peter said, "Lord, if it is You, tell me to come to You on the water."

Jesus told Peter to come. Peter got out of the boat. He began to walk on the water.

The wind started to blow. Peter was afraid. He began to sink. He called to Jesus, "Lord, save me!"

Jesus told Peter, "You do not have much faith. Why did you doubt Me?"

Jesus took Peter's hand. They climbed into the boat. The wind stopped blowing.

The disciples saw what happened. They said, "You are really the Son of God."

New Words to Learn!
disciple, faith, pray, sink

A Fish with Money in Its Mouth

A Fish with Money in Its Mouth

Matthew 17:24–27

Every year, people had to pay the temple tax. They had to give money to the tax collectors.

The tax collectors came to Peter. They asked him, "Doesn't your friend Jesus pay the temple tax?"

Peter answered, "Yes, He does."

Peter went into the house where Jesus was. Peter did not need to tell Jesus what the tax collector asked. Jesus already knew.

Jesus told Peter that His Father, God, was the Lord over all kings. Jesus said that He should not have to pay taxes.

But, Jesus did not want to make the tax collectors angry. He wanted to follow the king's laws. Jesus had a plan to get the money.

Jesus told Peter to go to the lake. He told Peter to put his fishing line into the water.

Jesus said, "Take the first fish that you catch. Open its mouth. You will find a coin. Take it and give it to the tax collector. It is enough money to pay My tax and yours."

New Words to Learn!
coin, collector, temple

The Lost Sheep

The Lost Sheep

Luke 15:1–7

A crowd gathered around Jesus. Jesus was being kind to the sinners in the group. Some people did not like that. They did not want to be near sinners. They said, "This man likes sinners. He even eats with them."

Jesus wanted the people to know that God loves everyone. God is happy when a person stops sinning. Jesus told the people a story to help them understand.

Jesus said, "A man has 100 sheep. What will he do if he loses one? Won't he look for the lost sheep?

"When he finds the lost sheep, he will be happy. He will put the sheep on his shoulders. He will take the sheep home.

"The man will tell his friends and neighbors the good news. He will say, 'I have found my lost sheep. I want to share my happiness with you.'"

Jesus told the crowd that God feels the same way. God is happy when a sinner finds his way back to God.

The Good Samaritan

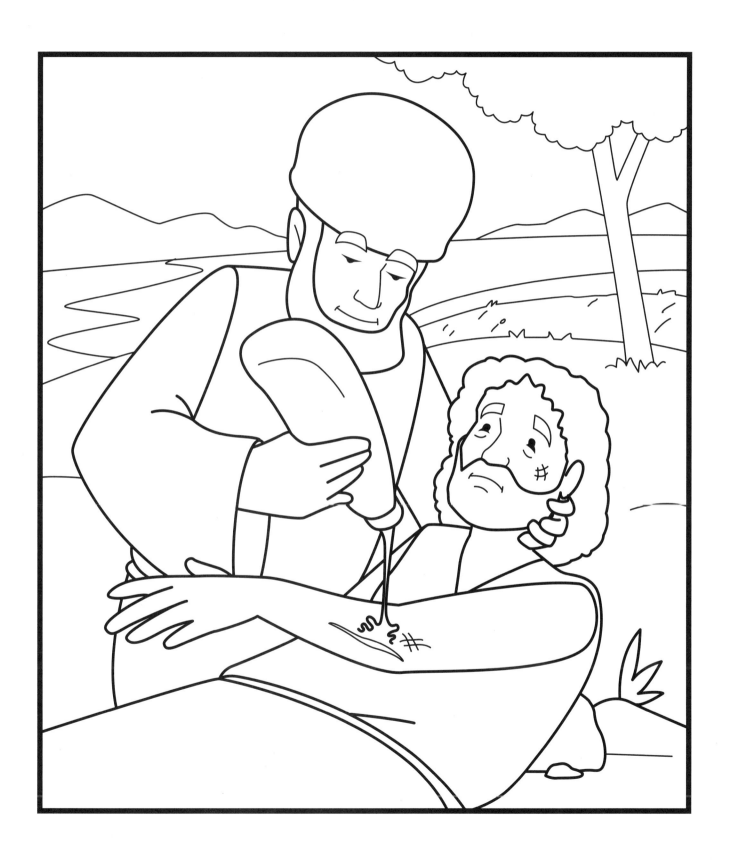

The Good Samaritan

Luke 10:25–37

Jesus was talking to a large group of people. A man asked Jesus, "What should I do to live forever in heaven?

Jesus answered, "What does the law say?"

The man said, "Love God with all your heart and with all your soul. Love Him with all your strength and with all your mind. Love your neighbor as much as you love yourself."

Jesus said, "Do this and you will live forever in heaven."

Then, the man asked, "Who is my neighbor?"

Jesus wanted the man to know that everyone is his neighbor. He told a story to help the man understand.

Jesus said, "A man was walking down the road. Robbers took everything that he had. They left him lying on the side of the road.

"A priest walked by. He saw the man. He crossed to the other side of the road. The priest did not help the man. Another person walked by. He did not help the man either.

"The next person who came by was a Samaritan. Some people did not like Samaritans. The Samaritan stopped to help.

"The Samaritan treated the hurt man like a neighbor. He used oil and wine to clean the man's cuts. He put the man on a donkey. He took the man to town. The Samaritan paid someone to take care of the man."

Then, Jesus asked, "Who was a good neighbor in this story?"

The man answered, "The man who stopped to help."

Jesus said, "You should be a good neighbor to others too."

. . . .

New Words to Learn!

forever, priest, soul

Jesus Visits Mary and Martha

Jesus Visits Mary and Martha

Luke 10:38–42

Jesus and His disciples went to many towns. They stayed at people's houses along the way.

In one town, there were two sisters who shared a house. Their names were Martha and Mary. Martha invited Jesus to come to their home.

Jesus went into the house. He sat down. Mary sat on the floor at Jesus' feet. She wanted to hear every word that Jesus said.

Martha did not sit and listen to Jesus. She was busy making the house ready for Jesus. Mary did not help her sister.

Martha went to Jesus. She said, "Don't You care that I am doing all of this work by myself? Tell Mary to help me."

Jesus said, "Martha, Martha. You should not worry about those things. Mary has chosen the right thing to do. She has chosen to be with Me. I will not take that away from her."

New Words to Learn!
chosen, disciple, invite

Jesus Helps a Blind Man

Jesus Helps a Blind Man

John 9:1–11

Jesus and His disciples were walking. They saw a man. He had been blind since he was born.

The disciples asked Jesus why the man was blind. They asked, "Is it because he sinned? Is it because his parents sinned?"

Jesus said, "No, this happened so that God can show His work. We must do God's work here."

Jesus spit in the dirt. He made mud. He put the mud on the man's eyes.

Jesus told the man to go to the water. He told the man to wash his eyes. The man did what Jesus said. He could see!

The man went home. He saw his neighbors. They asked, "Is this the same man who used to sit and beg?"

He said, "I am the same man. Jesus made some mud. He put it on my eyes. He told me to go to the water and wash my eyes. I went and washed. Then, I could see."

New Words to Learn!
blind, disciple, parent, spit

The Good Shepherd

The Good Shepherd

John 9:24–38, 10:1–18

Some people did not like what Jesus taught. They did not believe that Jesus was the Son of God. Jesus wanted them to know why God sent Him to earth. Jesus wanted them to know that He came to help people.

Jesus told the people a story to help them understand. He said, "A shepherd knows his sheep. He calls them by name. The sheep will follow their shepherd because they know his voice.

"I am like the gate for the sheep. I keep out anyone who comes to hurt the sheep. I will save everyone who believes in Me."

The people listened to the story. But, they did not understand. Jesus told another story.

Jesus said, "If a wolf tries to hurt the sheep, the shepherd will protect them. Someone else would run away from the wolf. But, a good shepherd will fight the wolf to save his sheep. I am the Good Shepherd. The people are My sheep."

Jesus was saying that He wants to protect all people because He loves them. He promises to keep everyone who believes in Him safe.

Some people did not believe Jesus. But, others put their faith in His words.

. . . .

New Words to Learn!
protect, shepherd

The Lost Son Comes Home

The Lost Son Comes Home

Luke 15:10–32

Jesus wanted people to know that God is happy when someone comes back to Him. Jesus told this story to help them understand.

Jesus said, "A man had two sons. The younger son asked for his share of everything that his father owned. The man gave each son half of everything.

"The young son moved far away. He spent his money quickly. Soon, he had no money. He got a job feeding pigs. The young son was hungry, but no one gave him any food.

"The young son wanted to go home. He wanted to be forgiven.

"His father saw his young son coming. He ran to him. He put his arms around his son and kissed him.

"The young son said, 'Father, I have sinned against heaven and you.' But, his father was not angry. He was happy to see his son. He made plans to have a party for his son.

"The older son was working in the fields. He heard music and dancing. A servant told him, 'Your brother has come home. He is safe. Your father is having a party.'

"The older son was angry. He told his father, 'For many years I have worked hard for you. I have listened to you. My brother left home. He wasted your money. Why are you having a party for him?'

"His father said, 'You are always with me. Everything that I have is yours. Your brother was lost. I thought that he was dead. Now he is found.'"

. . . .

New Word to Learn!
servant

Jesus Sees Zacchaeus

Jesus Sees Zacchaeus

Luke 19:1–10

People paid money to tax collectors every year. The tax collectors gave the money to the city. But, some tax collectors were bad people. They kept some of the money for themselves. Many people thought that tax collectors were sinners.

Zacchaeus was a tax collector. He was rich. Jesus was passing through Zacchaeus's city. A large crowd gathered to see Jesus.

Zacchaeus ran ahead of the crowd. He wanted to see Jesus too. Zacchaeus was a short man. So, he climbed a tree so that he could see Jesus better.

Jesus came to the place where Zacchaeus was. He looked at Zacchaeus in the tree. Jesus said, "Zacchaeus, come down. I will stay at your house today."

The crowd was surprised. They did not think that Jesus should visit a sinner's house. Zacchaeus was happy that Jesus was visiting him.

Zacchaeus told Jesus, "I will give half of everything that I have to poor people. If I have taken people's money, I will pay back more than I took." Jesus told Zacchaeus that God had forgiven him for the bad things that he had done.

New Word to Learn!
collector

Washing Feet

Washing Feet

John 13:1–17

Jesus knew that soon He would leave earth. It was almost time for Jesus to go to His Father in heaven.

Jesus was eating dinner with His disciples. When they finished eating, Jesus got up. He put a towel around His waist. He poured water into a large bowl. Jesus wanted to show His disciples that He loved them.

Peter asked Jesus, "Lord, are You about to wash my feet?" He did not think that the Son of God should wash feet!

Jesus said, "You do not understand what I am doing now. But, later you will understand." Jesus wanted to show Peter that people should do kind things for each other.

Then, Jesus washed each disciple's feet. He used the towel to dry them.

When Jesus finished, He asked His disciples, "Do you understand what I have done for you? I am your Lord and your Teacher. I have washed your feet. You should do for others as I have done for you."

Jesus was showing His disciples that one person is not more important than another person. Everyone is important.

Jesus said, "Now you know these things. You will be blessed if you do them."

New Words to Learn!
blessed, disciple, towel, waist

The Vine and the Branches

153

The Vine and the Branches

John 14:1–14, 15:5–12

The disciples knew that Jesus would be leaving them soon. Jesus said, "Do not be sad. Trust in God. Trust in Me too."

Jesus told the disciples that some day they would join Him in heaven. The disciples said that they did not know how to get to heaven.

Jesus said, "I am the truth and the life. I am the only way to the Father." Jesus was telling the disciples that if they believe in Him, they will go to heaven.

Jesus gave the disciples an important job to do after He was gone. He told them to keep teaching people about God.

Jesus told the disciples a story to help them understand. Jesus said, "God is like a gardener. A gardener wants his plants to grow good fruit. Fruit grows on branches that come from the vine. If a branch is cut from the vine, it will dry up and die. Fruit cannot grow if the branch dies."

Jesus said, "I am the vine, and you are the branches."

Jesus knew that the disciples could do many good things on earth. But, they must remember to keep close to Jesus, like the branches on a vine. Jesus promised to help the disciples, even after He went to heaven.

Jesus said, "Here is my command. Love each other as I have loved you."

New Words to Learn!
disciple, join

A Donkey for a King

A Donkey for a King

Mark 11:1–11

Jesus and the disciples were traveling to Jerusalem. Jesus told His disciples, "Go ahead of Me. Go to the next town. You will see a young donkey. It has never been ridden."

He told the disciples to untie the donkey. Jesus said to bring the donkey to Him.

The disciples found the donkey. They untied it. Some people asked, "Why are you doing that?"

The disciples said that Jesus wanted the donkey. The people let the disciples go.

The disciples gave the donkey to Jesus. They spread their coats on the donkey's back. Jesus sat on the donkey.

Jesus and the disciples traveled on. The people of Jerusalem were happy to see Jesus coming. Some people spread their coats on the road. Other people cut branches from the fields. They laid the branches on the road. The people were treating Jesus like a king.

Some people walked in front of Jesus. Others followed behind Him. They shouted, "Blessed is He who comes in the name of the Lord!"

New Words to Learn!
bless, disciple

The Last Supper

The Last Supper

Matthew 26:1–2, 26:14–30; Luke 22:7–20

Some people did not like Jesus. They wanted to get rid of Him. Jesus told His disciples, "After the Passover Feast, men will take Me away. I will be crucified."

A disciple named Judas went to the priests. The priests said, "We will pay you to give Jesus to us." Judas said that he would do it.

Two days later, Jesus was eating the Passover Feast with the disciples. Jesus said, "One of you will give Me to the men who will crucify Me."

Each disciple said sadly, "I am sure I will not give You to them."

Judas said, "I am sure that it is not me."

Jesus told him, "Yes, it is you."

Jesus picked up a piece of bread. He thanked God and broke the bread. He gave it to the disciples. Jesus said, "Take this and eat it. This is My body. I am giving it for you." Jesus meant that He would take away everyone's sins when He died.

Then, he picked up a cup. He thanked God and shared it with the disciples. Jesus said, "Drink from it, all of you. This is My blood of the new covenant. It will be poured out so that sins will be forgiven. Do this and remember Me."

Jesus wanted the disciples to know that He loved them. He would always be with them, even when He was in heaven.

New Words to Learn!
covenant, crucify, disciple, pour, priest

Jesus Is Crucified

Jesus Is Crucified

Luke 22:39–54, 23:1–46; Matthew 27:29

After the Last Supper, Jesus went outside to pray. His disciples followed Him. They went to sleep in the garden.

Jesus was waking them when a crowd came. The crowd did not like Jesus. They wanted to get rid of Him. They took Him to their ruler. His name was Pontius Pilate.

Pilate asked Jesus, "Are You the King of the Jews?"

Jesus said, "Yes, I am."

Pilate told the crowd that Jesus did not do anything wrong. Pilate sent Jesus to another ruler named King Herod. He also said that Jesus did not do anything wrong.

King Herod and his men made fun of Jesus. They dressed Him like a king. They gave Him a fancy robe. They put a crown of thorns on His head. Then, they sent Him back to Pilate.

Pilate said to the crowd, "Herod and I do not think that this man should die. I will punish Him. Then, I will let Him go."

The people wanted Jesus to die. They yelled, "Crucify Him! Crucify Him!" Pilate did what the crowd wanted. He gave the order to put Jesus on the cross.

People watched Jesus die. Some people laughed at Him. They said, "He saved others. Let Him save Himself."

Jesus prayed, "Father, forgive them. They do not know what they are doing."

The sun stopped shining. Jesus called out to God, "Father, I put Myself into Your hands." Jesus took His last breath.

New Words to Learn!

crucify, disciple, fancy, pray, robe, thorn

Jesus Is Not in the Tomb

Jesus Is Not in the Tomb

John 19:40–42, 20:1–23; Luke 23:53, 24:36–49

After Jesus died, two men wrapped His body in pieces of cloth. They laid Him in a tomb. The men sealed the tomb with a stone.

Three days later, Mary Magdalene went to the tomb. The stone had been moved. Mary ran to the disciples. She said, "They have taken Jesus. I don't know where they put Him."

Two disciples ran to the tomb. They saw the pieces of cloth. Jesus was not there. The disciples did not know that Jesus had risen from the dead. They went home.

Mary stayed outside of the tomb and cried. She looked into the tomb. She saw two angels dressed in white. They sat where Jesus had been. The angels asked Mary, "Why are you crying?"

Mary said, "They have taken away my Lord."

Mary saw a man standing near her. She did not know that the man was Jesus. Jesus asked Mary, "Who are you looking for?"

Mary looked at Him again. She said, "Teacher!" because she knew that He was Jesus.

Jesus said, "Go tell the disciples that I am going home to God."

Mary went to the disciples. She told them, "I have seen the Lord!"

Later that night, Jesus appeared to the disciples in a locked room. He said, "Peace be with you. The Father has sent Me. Now, I am sending you." Jesus was telling the disciples to teach about God.

Then, Jesus breathed on the disciples. He said, "Now you have the Holy Spirit. You can forgive people, and their sins will be taken away."

New Words to Learn!
angel, disciple, holy, tomb, wrap

Doubting Thomas

Bible Story Color 'n' Learn • CD-204073

Doubting Thomas

John 20:24–29

A few nights after Jesus died, the disciples gathered in a locked room. Jesus appeared in front of them. Thomas was not with the other disciples that night. Later, they told Thomas, "We have seen the Lord!"

Thomas thought that Jesus was still dead. Thomas told the other disciples, "I will not believe it until I see the marks on His hands."

The next week, Jesus appeared in the locked room again. This time, all of the disciples were there. Jesus said to them, "Peace be with you."

Then, Jesus showed Thomas the marks on His hands. He told Thomas to stop doubting and to start believing.

Thomas looked at the marks on Jesus' hands. Thomas said to Jesus, "My Lord and my God!"

Jesus said, "You believe that I am alive because you have seen Me. Blessed are the people who believe without seeing Me."

New Words to Learn!
alive, bless, disciple

Breakfast with Jesus

Breakfast with Jesus

John 21:1–14

Many days after Jesus died, Peter said, "I am going out on the boat to fish." Some of the other disciples went with him. They fished all night. They did not catch any fish.

The next morning, they saw a man. He was standing on the shore. They could not tell that He was Jesus.

The man asked them, "Friends, do you have any fish?"

They said, "No."

The man told them to throw the net on the right side of the boat. He told them that they would catch fish there.

The disciples did what the man said. They caught many fish. They could not lift the heavy net.

One disciple looked at the man on the shore again. He said, "It is the Lord!"

The disciple jumped into the water. The others followed him in the boat. The disciples dragged the net to the shore. It had more than 100 large fish in it.

The disciples reached the shore. They saw fish and bread cooking on a fire. Jesus said to them, "Come and have breakfast."

Jesus shared the bread and fish with the disciples. This was the third time that Jesus visited the disciples after He died.

New Words to Learn!
disciple, net

Peter's Second Chance

Peter's Second Chance

Matthew 26:34–35, 26:69–75; John 21:15–17

A few days before Jesus died, He told Peter, "The rooster will crow. Before it does, you will say three times that you do not know Me."

Peter thought that Jesus was wrong. He told Jesus, "I will never say that I do not know You."

Peter watched men take Jesus away. People asked Peter if he knew Jesus. Peter said three times, "I do not know Him."

Then, the rooster crowed. Peter cried. He was sad because he had lied. It happened just as Jesus said that it would.

Jesus visited the disciples after He died. He asked Peter, "Do you really love Me?"

Peter said, "Yes, Lord. You know that I love You."

Jesus said, "Feed my lambs."

Jesus asked Peter again, "Do you really love Me?"

Peter said, "Yes, Lord. You know that I love You."

Jesus told him, "Take care of My sheep."

Jesus asked the same question again. Peter said, "Lord, You know everything. You know that I love You."

Jesus said, "Feed My sheep."

Peter knew that Jesus was giving him a special job. Jesus wanted him to take care of the people who believed in Jesus.

. . . .

New Word to Learn!
disciple

God's Special Gift

God's Special Gift

Acts 1:1–9, 2:1–39

After Jesus died, He stayed on earth for 40 days. One day, Jesus visited the disciples as they were eating.

Jesus told the disciples, "Do not leave Jerusalem. Wait for the gift that My Father has promised. John baptized people with water. You will be baptized with the Holy Spirit."

Jesus told the disciples that they would receive a special gift. The Holy Spirit would come to give them special power. Then, the disciples could teach anywhere in the world. After Jesus said this, He was taken into the sky. A cloud covered Him.

The disciples were together in a house in Jerusalem. A loud sound came from heaven. It was like a strong wind. It filled the house.

Fire appeared from above. It was shaped like long ribbons or tongues. A tongue of fire touched each disciple. The disciples were filled with the Holy Spirit. They began speaking in languages that they had never spoken before.

Many people heard the sound and came to the house. The people asked, "How do these men know all of our languages?"

Peter told the people, "God has raised Jesus to life. He gave us the Holy Spirit that you see and hear."

The people asked Peter what they should do. Peter said, "First, you should be sorry for your sins. You should be baptized in the name of Jesus Christ. Then, you will receive the gift of the Holy Spirit. This is a promise to you and to everyone who believes in God."

. . . .

New Words to Learn!

baptize, disciple, holy, reward, ribbon, tongue

Jesus Chooses Saul

 Bible Story Color 'n' Learn • CD-204073

Jesus Chooses Saul

Acts 9:1–22

Saul put Christians in jail because they believed in Jesus. One day, Saul was walking to Damascus with his friends. They were looking for Christians to put in jail. Suddenly, a bright light from heaven flashed around Saul. He fell to the ground.

Saul heard a voice. It said, "Saul, why are you against Me?"

Saul asked, "Who are you, Lord?"

The voice answered, "I am Jesus. I am the One you are against." Jesus told Saul to go to the city and wait.

Saul's friends heard the voice too. But, they did not see anyone.

Saul stood up. He opened his eyes. But, he could not see.

Saul's friends led him to Damascus. Saul was blind for three days. He did not eat or drink anything.

Jesus sent a disciple to help Saul. Jesus told the disciple, "Go to Saul. I have chosen him to teach My word to all people, even kings."

The disciple went to Saul. He told Saul, "The light that you saw was the Lord Jesus. He has sent me to help you see again."

The disciple placed his hands on Saul. Saul could see again. He was filled with the Holy Spirit. Saul stood up and was baptized.

Saul began preaching in Damascus. He told people that Jesus is the Son of God. They said, "Is this Saul? Is this the same man who took Christians to jail?" They were amazed how Saul had changed.

New Words to Learn!
amaze, baptize, blind, choose, Christian, disciple, holy, jail, preach

An Angel Frees Peter

173

An Angel Frees Peter

Acts 12:1–17

King Herod did not like Christians. He told his men to put Christians in prison. The men killed some of the Christians.

James was one of Jesus' disciples. King Herod told his men to kill James. King Herod saw that this made the Jewish people happy. So, King Herod put the disciple Peter in prison. Four men guarded Peter all of the time.

Christians knew that Peter was in prison. They prayed for God to help him.

One night, Peter was sleeping between two soldiers. He had chains around his wrists. Two guards stood by the door.

Suddenly, an angel appeared in a bright light. The angel woke up Peter. The angel said, "Quick! Get up!" Peter's chains broke and fell to the ground.

The angel told Peter, "Put on your sandals. Put on your coat and follow me."

Peter thought that he was dreaming. The angel led him past the guards. The heavy gate of the city opened by itself. Peter walked down the road. Then, the angel left him.

Peter went to a friend's house. He knocked on the door. Many people were inside. They were praying for God to save Peter.

A servant opened the door. She told the people, "Peter is at the door!"

The people were surprised. They were happy to see Peter. He told them how the Lord had sent an angel to free him from prison.

. . . .

New Words to Learn!

angel, chain, Christian, disciple, pray, prison, sandals, servant, soldier, wrist

Jesus Will Return

Bible Story Color 'n' Learn • CD-204073

Jesus Will Return

Revelation 1:1–2, 1:9–18, 21:1–27; 22:7–21

John was one of Jesus' disciples. After Jesus died, John taught God's Word. This made the ruler angry. When John grew older, he was put in prison.

One day, John heard a loud voice. It was like a trumpet. The voice told John to write down everything that he saw.

Then, John saw who was speaking. It was a man with white hair. He was wearing a long robe.

The man told John, "Do not be afraid. I am the Living One. I was dead. Now, I am alive forever." John knew that He was Jesus.

John saw a new heaven and a new earth. Jesus said, "God will live with the people. God will wipe away their tears. There will be no pain or death."

John saw seven angels. One angel said, "You can believe my words. God has sent me to show you the future."

The angel showed John a city of gold and jewels coming from heaven. The main street of the city was gold.

A river flowed from the throne of God to the city. The water flowed into the middle of the street.

John heard a voice say, "I am coming soon! I will judge each person for what he has done. Some will come into the Holy City. Some will stay outside. I am Jesus. I am the Son of David."

John said, "Amen. Come, Lord Jesus!" John knew that Jesus would return to earth some day.

. . . .

New Words to Learn!

alive, amen, angel, disciple, forever, holy, jewel, main, prison, robe, throne